CALIFORNIA
THEN AND NOW®
People and Places

CALIFORNIA

THEN AND NOW®
People and Places

Karl Mondon

First published in the United Kingdom in 2013 by
PAVILION BOOKS
43 Great Ormond Street,
London WC1N 3HZ

© Pavilion Books, 2013

Reprinted 2014 (twice), 2018

Project Manager: Frank Hopkinson

ISBN: 978-1-86205-994-8

A CIP catalogue record for this book is available from the British Library.

Printed by 1010 Printing International Limited, China.

SAN FRANCISCO
page 8

LOS ANGELES
RIVERSIDE
SANTA BARBARA
page 174

CATALINA ISLAND
page 322

SAN DIEGO
page 350

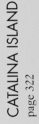

Then and Now – it's a much-loved concept, used to show how a location has changed over the years. In some cases a span of 100 years can show very little change to the scene; Mission Alcala near San Diego has had a coat of paint and more flowers, but little else is different a century later. With Cliff House in San Francisco there have been five distinct buildings over the years, all of which we feature in this book.

But whereas a conventional 'Then and Now' shows you a 'Then' followed by a 'Now,' *California Then and Now – People and Places* mixes up the format, sometimes showing a number of different 'Thens' and a single 'Now,' sometimes showing a single 'Then' and multiple 'Nows.' This allows the reader to see aspects of a historic location that are impossible to replicate today, often through the growth of trees, or the addition of new buildings to the old.

San Francisco-based photographer Karl Mondon tracked down the old locations and even went up in a helicopter to get some key images for the book which highlights the very best of California's great cities.

SAN
FRAN

CISCO

The third Cliff House, c. 1905

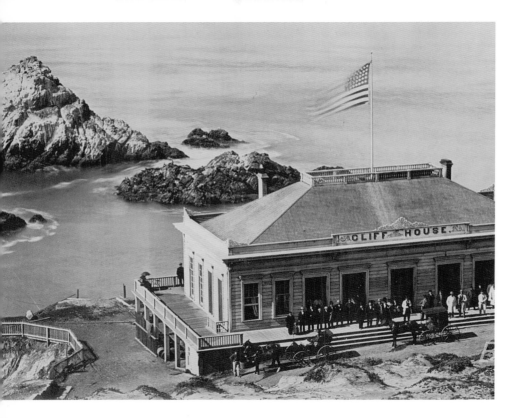

The enlarged first Cliff House, c. 1877

The fourth Cliff House, c. 1956

The second Cliff House, c. 1880

The third Cliff House ablaze, September 1, 1907

California Street, April 28, 1922

Fairmont Hotel after the Great Fire of 1906

Fairmont Hotel

View from Ferry Building, 1906

019244. RUSSIAN AND TELEGRAPH HILLS FROM ROOF OF FERRY BO. SAN FRANCISCO, CAL.

The "Evening Rush Hour" at the Ferry Building, 1915

San Francisco Maritime Museum, Beach Street, c. 1980

Powell Street looking south from Nob Hill, c. 1948

Grateful Dead at Haight Ashbury, 1967

From Saint Francis Yacht Club looking toward Marina Blvd, c. 1955

Looking north from Broadway down Baker Street, c. 1951

Looking North on Kearney Street, c. 1955

Broadway and Montgomery looking toward Russian Hill, April, 1944

View from Mount Olympus, c. 1951

Gay Pride, the Castro District, 2012

59

Looking North on Noe Street from near Liberty Street, c. 1955

View from Twin Peaks, c. 1955

Sentinel Building, c. 1962

Diamond Heights, c. 1951

Palace of Fine Arts renovation, 1964

The Ferry Building and Bay Bridge, c. 1960

Hobart Building on Market Street, c. 1966

700 Block, Market Street, c. 1966

800 Block, Market Street, c. 1966

Looking south on Montgomery from Green Street, c. 1951

Grant Avenue, Chinatown, c. 1965

Looking north on Kearney Street at Market Street, c. 1892

Hyde Street looking north at Union, c. 1951

Fisherman's Wharf, c. 1957

Grant Avenue, Chinatown, c. 1952

2500 block of Jackson Street, Pacific Heights, c. 1952

Market Street, c. 1955

The Presidio of San Francisco, Crissy Field and Fort Point, 1930

Latham flying over the Golden Gate, c. 1911

Golden Gate Bridge, July 1934

The Golden Gate and Fort Point, c. 1925

Golden Gate Bridge from the south

Golden Gate Bridge, c. 2005

Golden Gate Bridge from the north, c. 1975

Golden Gate Bridge at sunset

Golden Gate Bridge, 75th Anniversary fireworks, 2012

Alvord Lake and tunnel, Golden Gate Park, 1892

Golden Gate Park Conservatory illustration, 1886

Alcatraz Island, 1928

Alcatraz Island, c. 1978

Alcatraz Island

The burned out Officers' Club on Alcatraz Island, c. 2005

Yerba Buena Island, the Naval Station is at bottom right, 1936

Yerba Buena Island and Bay Bridge, 1998

Bay Bridges, 2012

A "slave girl in holiday attire," Chinatown, c. 1900

"A family from the Consulate," Chinatown, c. 1900

Balclutha, renamed Star of Alaska, 1913

SEASON 1913.

CAPTAIN, 1ST MATE,
SUPT AND STORE KEEPER,
© A.P. Ass'n CANNERY, SHIP STAR OF ALASKA.

Balclutha, restored and berthed at Hyde Street Pier, c. 1978

Restored Scow *Alma*, Hyde Street Pier

Ferry *San Mateo*, Hyde Street Pier, 1922 and Ferry *Eureka*

168

Historic ships at Hyde Street Pier

Hawaiian-themed cable car, c. 1953

LOS AN
RIVERSIDE
SANTA

GELES

BARBARA

Los Angeles Public Library at Los Angeles City Hall, c. 1905

MEZZANINE
FLOOR

Los Angeles City Hall, Third Floor Council Chambers, 1997

Vine Street near Broadway Plaza Hotel, c. 1955

Vine near Sunset, Los Angeles, c. 1945

Coca Cola Bottling Plant, 1334 South Central Avenue, Los Angeles, c. 1974

Thomas Jefferson High School, Los Angeles, c. 1970

2525 Main Street, Los Angeles, c. 1970

Union Market, 1530–1536 West Sixth Street, Los Angeles, c. 1971

The (1936) Merle Norman Building, Los Angeles

Ralph's, Westwood Village, c. 1954

Angels Flight, Los Angeles, c. 1959

224

99691 DEPARTURE OF THE OVERLAND, LOS ANGELES, CAL.

Union Station, Los Angeles, c. 1947

Union Station, Los Angeles, c. 1947

Long Beach Pier and bathers, 1905

Copyright 1 By G.C.Ho[...]

Long Beach Pier and promenade, 1905

Long Beach auditorium and Majestic Dance Hall, 1909

HOTEL VIRGINIA, LONG BEACH, CAL.

RMS *Queen Mary*, Long Beach

San Pedro harbor, c. 1900

USS *Iowa*, San Pedro

THE
MOUNT LOWE RAILWAY
1893 - 1936
HAS BEEN PLACED ON THE
NATIONAL REGISTER
OF HISTORIC PLACES
BY THE UNITED STATES
DEPARTMENT OF THE INTERIOR
1993

The Arroyo Seco Bridge, Pasadena, c. 1926

Railway station, Pasadena, c. 1904

BUSCH·GARDEN
COPYRIGHT
1909
BY
HAROLD A. PARKER

Busch Garden, Pasadena, 1909

264

Rose Bowl, Pasadena, c. 1990

Rose Bowl, Pasadena, 1934

Olympic bicycle track, view south, Rose Bowl, Pasadena, 1932

276

Glenwood Mission Inn, Riverside, c. 1910

Union Pacific railroad bridge across Santa Anna River, Riverside, c. 1904

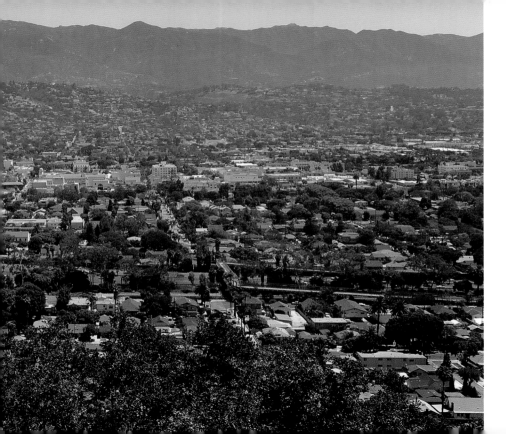

Santa Barbara, c. 1906

Mission Santa Barbara, 2201 Laguna Street, Santa Barbara, 1917

C.H.CRONISE.

Hotel Potter, Santa Barbara, 1909

Site of Hotel Potter's grounds, Santa Barbara

Santa Monica Pier, 2009

"DEATH" CURVE, A RIGHT ANGLED
TURN WHERE DANGER LURKS

AVENUE

BRIDGE

WILSHIRE

"Death Curve" on Wilshire Boulevard, Santa Monica, 1914

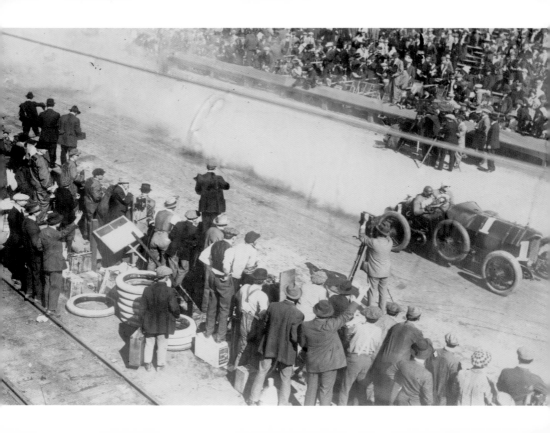

The start and finish of the Vanderbilt Cup race, Santa Monica, 1914

Los Angeles Motorcycle Club, Venice, 1911

Los Angeles Motorcycle Club, Venice, 1911

Hotel St. Mark, Venice, c. 1910

Archery practice in front of Royce Hall, UCLA, Los Angeles, c. 1952

CATA

LINA
ISLAND

A "fishermaiden and her catch," Avalon Harbor, 1906

Edward Llewellen with World Record Black Sea Bass, (425 lbs.), 1903

John I. Perkins with World Record Black Sea Bass, (428 lbs.), 1905

CATALINA

Now see Santa Catalina the Scenic Ri...

of the USA ...yet only a short delightful voyage from Los An...

Catalina Island poster, c. 1935 and visitors arriving, c. 1910

Avalon Pier, c. 1910

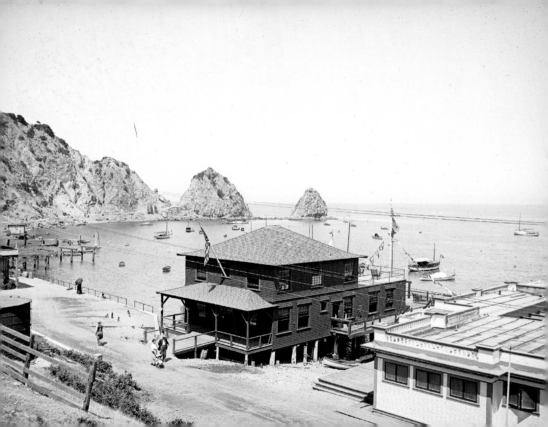

Tuna Club clubhouse, c. 1910

"Staging at Catalina Island," 1909

Staging at Catalina Isl. Cal.

Copyrighted, 1909
by
P.V. Reyes
Avalon
Cal.

336

342

"Pleasure boating" in Avalon Harbor, c. 1910

Hotel Metropole, Avalon, c. 1901

Pleasure submarining and electric buggies, Avalon

SAN

DIEGO

Old Town sign, San Diego, 1940

Jose Antonio Estudillo House, Old Town, San Diego, 1936

CAL. 4

Santa Fe Railroad, Kettner Boulevard, San Diego, 1914

360

AND CORONADO BEACH, CAL.

USS *Midway* Museum, San Diego

Sidewalk opposite the U.S. Grant Hotel, San Diego, 1941

Horton House Hotel, San Diego, c. 1880

383

Hotel del Coronado, Coronado Beach, c. 1910

Hotel del Coronado, Coronado Beach, 1941

Point Loma Lighthouse, c. 1890

Spiral staircase, Point Loma Lighthouse

ibit

Seen by over...
One Million Visitors

Modeltown in Balboa Park, San Diego, 1935

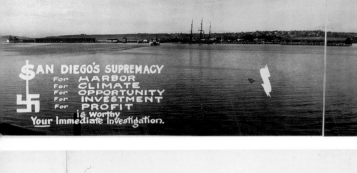

$SAN DIEGO'S SUPREMACY
For HARBOR
For CLIMATE
For OPPORTUNITY
For INVESTMENT
For PROFIT
IS Worthy
Your Immediate Investigation.

San Diego the Beautiful
"The View Poi~
WE PAY YOUR FARE. —— IF YOU

San Diego the Beautiful,
WE PAY YOUR FARE —— IF YOU BUY FROM US.

SELECT HOME SITES
In The Ideal Homeland
on small monthly payments.
939 - 6th St. San Diego.
HOMELAND
IMPROVEMENT CO.
208 Pacific Electric Bldg,
Los Angeles.

orld"
dley Warner)
ROM US.

"POINT OF THE WORLD."
(Chas. Dudley Warner.)

SELECT HOME SITES
In the ideal homeland
on small monthly payments.
939 - 6th St. San Diego.
HOMELAND
IMPROVEMENT CO.
208 Pacific Electric Bldg. Lios A.